Anthony Benezet

A Caution and Warning to Great Britain

Anthony Benezet

A Caution and Warning to Great Britain

ISBN/EAN: 9783348070225

Printed in Europe, USA, Canada, Australia, Japan

Cover: Foto ©Suzi / pixelio.de

More available books at **www.hansebooks.com**

A CAUTION

TO

GREAT BRITAIN

AND

Her COLONIES,

IN

A short REPRESENTATION of The CALAMITOUS STATE of the ENSLAVED NEGROES In the BRITISH DOMINIONS.

By ANT. BENEZET.

PHILADELPHIA. Printed:
LONDON Reprinted, 1767.

A
CAUTION, &c.

AT a time when the general rights and liberties of mankind, and the prefervation of thofe valuable privileges tranfmitted to us from our anceftors, are become fo much the fubjects of univerfal confideration; can it be an inquiry indifferent to any, how many of thofe who diftinguifh themfelves as the Advocates of Liberty, remain infenfible and inattentive to the treatment of thoufands and tens of thoufands of our fellow men, who, from motives of avarice, and the inexorable degree of tyrant cuftom, are at this very time kept in the moft deplorable ftate of Slavery, in many parts of the *Britifh* Dominions?

The intent of publifhing the following fheets, is more fully to make known the aggravated iniquity attending the practice of the Slave-Trade; whereby many thoufands of our fellow-creatures, as free as ourfelves by nature, and equally with us the fubjects of Chrift's

Chrift's redeeming Grace, are yearly brought into inextricable and barbarous bondage; and many, very many, to miferable and untimely ends.

The Truth of this lamentable Complaint is fo obvious to perfons of candour, under whofe notice it hath fallen, that feveral have lately publifhed their fentiments thereon, as a matter which calls for the moft ferious confideration of all who are concerned for the civil or religious Welfare of their Country. How an evil of fo deep a dye, hath fo long, not only paffed uninterrupted by thofe in Power, but hath even had their Countenance, is indeed furprifing, and charity would fuppofe, muft in a great meafure have arifen from this, that many perfons in government, both of the Clergy and Laity, in whofe power it hath been to put a ftop to the Trade, have been unacquainted with the corrupt motives which gives life to it; and the groans, the dying groans, which daily afcend to God, the common Father of mankind, from the broken hearts of thofe his deeply oppreffed creatures; otherwife the powers of the earth would not, I think I may venture to fay, could not, have fo long authorized a practice fo inconfiftent with every idea of liberty and juftice, which, as the learned *James Fofter* fays, *Bids that God, which is the God and Father of the* Gentiles, *unconverted to* Chriftianity, *moft daring and*

and bold defiance; and spurns at all the principles both of natural and revealed Religion.

Much might justly be said of the temporal evils which attend this practice, as it is destructive of the welfare of human society, and of the peace and prosperity of every country, in proportion as it prevails. It might be also shewn, that it destroys the bonds of natural affection and interest, whereby mankind in general are united; that it introduces idleness, discourages marriage, corrupts the youth, ruins and debauches morals, excites continual apprehensions of dangers, and frequent alarms, to which the Whites are necessarily exposed from so great an encrease of a People, that, by their Bondage and Oppressions, become natural enemies, yet, at the same time, are filling the places and eating the bread of those who would be the Support and Security of the Country. But as these and many more reflections of the same kind, may occur to a considerate mind, I shall only endeavour to shew, from the nature of the Trade, the plenty which *Guiney* affords its inhabitants, the barbarous Treatment of the Negroes, and the Observations made thereon by Authors of note, that it is inconsistent with the plainest Precepts of the Gospel, the dictates of reason, and every common sentiment of Humanity.

In

In an Account of the *European* Settlements in *America*, printed in *London*, 1757, the Author speaking on this Subject, says: 'The Negroes in our Colonies endure a Slavery more compleat and attended with far worse circumstances than what any people in their condition suffer in any other part of the world, or have suffered in any other period of time: Proofs of this are not wanting. The prodigious waste which we experience in this unhappy part of our Species, is a full and melancholly Evidence of this Truth. The Island of *Barbadoes* (the Negroes upon which do not amount to eighty thousand) notwithstanding all the means which they use to encrease them by Propagation, and that the Climate is in every respect (except that of being more wholsome) exactly resembling the Climate from whence they come; notwithstanding all this, *Barbadoes* lies under a necessity of an annual recuit of five thousand slaves, to keep up the stock at the number I have mentioned. This prodigious failure, which is at least in the same proportion in all our Islands, shews demonstratively that some uncommon and unsupportable Hardship lies upon the Negroes, which wears them down in such a surprising manner; and this, I imagine, is principally the excessive labour which they undergo.'

In an Account of part of *North-America*, published by *Thomas Jeffery*, printed 1761,

speaking

speaking of the usage the Negroes receive in the *West-India* Islands, thus expresses himself: 'It's impossible for a human heart to
'reflect upon the servitude of these dregs of
'mankind, without in some measure feeling
'for their misery, which ends but with their
'lives.—— Nothing can be more wretched
'than the condition of this People. One
'would imagine, they were framed to be
'the disgrace of the human species, banished
'from their Country, and deprived of that
'blessing Liberty, on which all other nations
'set the greatest value, they are in a manner
'reduced to the condition of beasts of bur-
'den: In general a few roots, potatoes
'especially, are their food, and two rags;
'which neither screen them from the heat
'of the day, nor the extraordinary coolness
'of the night, all their covering; their sleep
'very short; their labour almost continual;
'they receive no wages, but have twenty
'lashes for the smallest fault.'

A considerate young person who was late in one of our *West-India* Islands, where he observed the miserable situation of the Negroes, makes the following remarks: 'I meet
'with daily exercise, to see the treatment
'which these miserable wretches meet with
'from their masters, with but few exceptions.
'They whip them most unmercifully, on
'small occasions; they beat them with thick
'Clubs,

' Clubs, and you will fee their Bodies all
' whaled and fcarred: in fhort, they feem to
' fet no other value on their lives than as they
' coft them fo much money; and are not
' reftrained from killing them, when angry,
' by a worthier confideration than that they
' lofe fo much. They act as tho' they did
' not look upon them as a race of human
' creatures, who have reafon, and remem-
' brance of misfortunes, but as beafts, like
' oxen, who are ftubborn, hardy and fenfe-
' lefs; fit for burdens, and defigned to bear
' them. They won't allow them to have any
' claim to human privileges, or fcarce, indeed,
' to be regarded as the work of God. Tho'
' it was confiftent with the juftice of our
' Maker to pronounce the fentence on our
' common parent, and through him on all
' fucceeding generations, *That he and they*
' *fhould eat their bread by the fweat of their*
' *brow*; yet does it not ftand recorded by the
' fame Eternal Truth, *That the Labourer is*
' *worthy of his Hire?* It cannot be allowed in
' natural juftice, that there fhould be a fervi-
' tude without condition: A cruel endlefs
' fervitude. It cannot be reconcileable to na-
' tural juftice, that whole nations, nay whole
' continents of men, fhould be devoted to do
' the drudgery of life for others, be dragged
' away from their attachments of relations
' and focieties, and made to ferve the appe-
' tites and pleafures of a race of men whofe
                                    ' fuperiority

' superiority has been obtained by an illegal
' force.'

A particular account of the treatment these
unhappy *Africans* receive in the *West-Indies*
was lately published, which even by those
who, blinded by interest, seek excuses for the
Trade, and endeavour to palliate the cruelty
exercised upon them, is allowed to be a true,
tho' rather too favourable representation of the
usage they receive, which is as follows, *viz.*
' The iniquity of the Slave-trade is greatly
' aggravated by the inhumanity with which
' the Negroes are treated in the Plantations,
' as well with respect to food and cloathing,
' as from the unreasonable labour which is
' commonly exacted from them. To which
' may be added the cruel chastisements they
' frequently suffer, without any other bounds
' than the will and wrath of their hard task-
' masters. In *Barbadoes*, and some other of
' the Islands, six pints of *Indian* corn and
' three herrings are reckoned a full week's
' allowance for a working slave, and in the
' System of Geography it is said, *That in* Ja-
' maica *the owners of the Negroe-slaves, set
' aside for each a parcel of ground, and allow
' them* Sundays *to manure it, the produce of
' which,* with sometimes a few herrings, or
' other salt-fish, *is all that is allowed for their
' support.* Their allowance for cloathing in
' the Islands is seldom more than six yards of
' ofenbrigs

'osenbrigs each year: And in the more north-
'ern Colonies, where the piercing westerly
'winds are long and sensibly felt, these poor
'*Africans* suffer much for want of sufficient
'cloathing, indeed some have none till they
'are able to pay for it by their labour. The
'time that the Negroes work in the *West-*
'*Indies*, is from day-break till noon; then
'again from two o' clock till dusk: (during
'which time they are attended by overseers,
'who severely scourge those who appear to
'them dilatory) and before they are suffered
'to go to their quarters, they have still some-
'thing to do, as collecting of herbage for
'the horses, gathering fuel for the boilers, &c.
'so that it is often half past twelve before
'they can get home, when they have scarce
'time to grind and boil their *Indian* corn;
'whereby it often happens that they are called
'again to labour before they can satisfy their
'Hunger: and here no delay or excuse will
'avail, for if they are not in the Field im-
'mediately upon the usual notice, they must
'expect to feel the Overseers Lash. In crop-
'time (which lasts many months) they are
'obliged (by turns) to work most of the night
'in the boiling-house. Thus their Owners,
'from a desire of making the greatest gain
'by the labour of their slaves, lay heavy
'Burdens on them, and yet feed and clothe
'them very sparingly, and some scarce feed or
'clothe them at all, so that the poor creatures

'are

'are obliged to shift for their living in the
' best manner they can, which occasions their
' being often killed in the neighbouring lands,
' stealing potatoes, or other food, to satisfy
' their hunger. And if they take any thing
' from the plantation they belong to, tho'
' under such pressing want, their owners will
' correct them severely, for taking a little of
' what they have so hardly laboured for,
' whilst they themselves riot in the greatest
' luxury and excess.—It is a matter of asto-
' nishment, how a people who, as a nation,
' are looked upon as generous and humane,
' and so much value themselves for their
' uncommon sense of the Benefit of Liberty,
' can live in the practice of such extreme op-
' pression and inhumanity, without seeing the
' inconsistency of such conduct, and without
' feeling great Remorse: Nor is it less amazing
' to hear these men calmly making calculations
' about the strength and lives of their fellow-
' men; in *Jamaica*, if six in ten, of the new
' imported Negroes survive the seasoning, it
' is looked upon as a gaining purchase: And
' in most of the other plantations, if the
' Negroes live eight or nine years, their labour
' is reckoned a sufficient compensation for
' their cost.——If calculations of this sort
' were made upon the strength and labour of
' beasts of burden it would not appear so
' strange, but even then a merciful man would
' certainly use his beast with more mercy than

' is

'is usually shewn to the poor Negroes.—Will
'not the groans of this deeply afflicted and
'oppressed people reach Heaven, and when
'the cup of iniquity is full, must not the
'inevitable consequence be pouring forth of
'the judgments of God upon their oppressors.
'But, alas! is it not too manifest that this
'oppression has already long been the object
'of the divine displeasure; for what heavier
'judgment, what greater calamity can befall
'any people, than to become a prey to that
'hardness of heart, that forgetfulness of God,
'and insensibility to every religious impres-
'sion; as well as that general depravation of
'manners, which so much prevails in the
'Colonies, in proportion as they have more or
'less enriched themselves, at the expence of
'the blood and bondage of the Negroes.'

The situation of the Negroes in our Southern provinces on the Continent, is also feelingly set forth by *George Whitefield*, in a Letter from *Georgia*, to the Inhabitants of *Maryland, Virginia, North* and *South-Carolina*, printed in the Year 1739, of which the following is an extract: 'As I lately passed
'through your provinces, in my way hither,
'I was sensibly touched with a fellow-feeling
'of the miseries of the poor Negroes. Whe-
'ther it be lawful for *Christians* to buy slaves,
'and thereby encourage the Nations from
'whom they are bought, to be at perpetual

wa

'war with each other, I shall not take upon
' me to determine; sure I am, it is sinful,
' when bought, to use them as bad, nay worse
' than as tho' they were brutes; and what-
' ever particular exception there may be, (as
' I would charitably hope there are some) I
' fear the generality of you, that own Negroes,
' are liable to such a charge; for your slaves,
' I believe, work as hard, if not harder, than
' the horses whereon you ride: These, after
' they have done their work, are fed and
' taken proper care of; but many Negroes,
' when wearied with labour, in your planta-
' tions, have been obliged to grind their own
' corn, after they return home. Your dogs
' are caressed and fondled at your tables; but
' your slaves, who are frequently stiled dogs
' or beasts, have not an equal privilege; they
' are scarce permitted to pick up the crumbs
' which fall from their master's table. — Not
' to mention what numbers have been given
' up to the inhuman usage of cruel task-
' masters, who, by their unrelenting scourges,
' have ploughed their backs, and made long
' furrows, and at length brought them even
' to death. When passing along, I have view-
' ed your plantations cleared and cultivated,
' many spacious houses built, and the owners
' of them faring sumptuously every day, my
' blood has frequently almost run cold within
' me, to consider how many of your slaves had
' neither convenient food to eat, or proper
       ' raiment

' raiment to put on, notwithstanding most of
' the comforts you enjoy were solely owing to
' their indefatigable labours.—The Scripture
' says, *Thou shalt not muzzle the ox that
' treadeth out the corn.* Does God take care
' for oxen ? and will he not take care of the
' Negroes also ? undoubtedly he will.—Go to
' now ye rich men, weep and howl for your
' miseries that shall come upon you : Behold
' the provision of the poor Negroes, who have
' reaped down your fields, which is by you
' denied them, crieth ; and the cries of them
' which reaped, are entred into the ears of
' the Lord of Sabbath. We have a remark-
' able instance of God's taking cognizance of,
' and avenging the quarrel of poor slaves,
' 2 Sam. xxi. 1. *There was a famine in the
' days of* David *three years, year after year* ;
' *and* David *enquired of the Lord : And the
' Lord answered, It is for* Saul, *and for his
' bloody house, because he slew the* Gibeonites.
' Two things are here very remarkable : First,
' These *Gibeonites* were only hewers of wood
' and drawers of water, or in other words,
' slaves like yours. Secondly, That this plague
' was sent by God many years after the injury,
' the cause of the plague, was committed.
' And for what end were this and such like
' examples recorded in holy Scriptures ? with-
' out doubt, for our learning.—For God is the
' same to-day, as he was yesterday, and will
' continue the same for ever. He does not
  ' reject

' reject the prayer of the poor and deftitute;
' nor difregard the cry of the meaneft Negro.
' The blood of them fpilt for thefe many
' years in your refpective provinces will afcend
' up to heaven againft you.'

Some who have only feen Negroes in an abject ftate of flavery, broken-fpirited and dejected, knowing nothing of their fituation in their native country, may apprehend, that they are naturally unfenfible of the benefits of Liberty, being deftitute and miferable in every refpect, and that our fuffering them to live amongft us (as the *Gibeonites* of old were permitted to live with the *Ifraelites*) tho' even on more oppreffive terms, is to them a favour; but thefe are certainly erroneous opinions, with refpect to far the greateft part of them: Altho' it is highly probable that in a country which is more than three thoufand miles in extent from north to fouth, and as much from eaft to weft, there will be barren parts, and many inhabitants more uncivilized and barbarous than others; as is the cafe in all other countries: Yet, from the moft authentic accounts, the inhabitants of *Guiney* appear, generally fpeaking, to be an induftrious, humane, fociable people, whofe capacities are naturally as enlarged, and as open to improvement, as thofe of the *Europeans*; and that their Country is fruitful, and in many places well improved, abounding in cattle, grain and
fruits:

fruits: And as the earth yields all the year round a fresh supply of food, and but little cloathing is requisite, by reason of the continual warmth of the climate; the necessaries of life are much easier procured in most parts of *Africa*, than in our more northern climes. This is confirmed by many authors of note, who have resided there; among others *M. Adanson*, in his account of *Goree* and *Senegal*, in the year 1754, says, ' Which way soever
' I turned my eyes on this pleasant spot, I
' beheld a perfect image of pure nature; an
' agreeable solitude, bounded on every side by
' charming landscapes, the rural situation of
' cottages in the midst of trees; the ease and
' indolence of the Negroes reclined under the
' shade of their spreading foliage; the simpli-
' city of their dress and manners; the whole
' revived in my mind the idea of our first
' parents, and I seemed to contemplate the
' world in its primitive state: They are, gene-
' rally speaking, very good-natured, sociable
' and obliging. I was not a little pleased with
' this my first reception; it convinced me,
' that there ought to be a considerable abate-
' ment made in the accounts I had read and
' heard every where of the savage character of
' the *Africans*. I observed, both in Negroes
' and Moors, great humanity and sociableness,
' which gave me strong hopes, that I should
' be very safe amongst them, and meet with
the

'the success I desired, in my inquiries after
'the curiosities of the country.'

William Bosman, a principal Factor for the *Dutch*, who resided sixteen years in *Guiney*, speaking of the natives of that part, where he then was, says, 'They are generally a good 'sort of People, honest in their dealings;' others he describes as 'being generally friendly 'to strangers, of a mild conversation, affable 'and easy to be overcome with reason.' He adds, 'That some Negroes, who have had 'an agreeable education, have manifested a 'brightness of understanding equal to any of 'us.' Speaking of the fruitfulness of the country, he says, 'It was very populous, 'plentifully provided with corn, potatoes and 'fruit, which grew close to each other; in 'some places a foot-path is the only ground 'that is not covered with them; the Negroes 'leaving no place, which is thought fertile, 'uncultivated; and immediately after they 'have reaped, they are sure to sow again.' Other parts he describes, as 'being full of 'towns and villages; the soil very rich, and 'so well cultivated as to look like an entire 'garden, abounding in rice, corn, oxen and 'poultry, and the inhabitants laborious.'

William Smith, who was sent by the *African* Company to visit their settlements on the coast of *Guiney*, in the year 1726, gives much the fame account of the country of *Delmina* and *Cape Corſe*, &c. for beauty and goodneſs, and adds, 'The more you come downward 'towards that part, called *Slave-Coaſt*, the 'more delightful and rich the ſoil appears.' Speaking of their diſpoſition, he ſays, 'They 'were a civil, good-natured people, induſtri-'ous to the laſt degree. It is eaſy to perceive 'what happy memories they are bleſſed with; 'and how great progreſs they would make in 'the ſciences, in caſe their genius was culti-'vated with ſtudy.' He adds, from the information he received of one of the Factors, who had reſided ten Years in that country: 'That the diſcerning natives account it their 'greateſt unhappineſs, that they were ever 'viſited by the *Europeans*. — That the *Chriſ-*'*tians* introduced the traffick of Slaves; and 'that before our coming they lived in peace.'

Andrew Brue, a principal man in the *French* Factory, in the account he gives of the great river *Senegal*, which runs many hundred miles up the country, tells his readers, 'The 'farther you go from the Sea, the country on 'the river ſeems more fruitful and well im-'proved. It abounds in *Guiney* and *Indian* 'corn, rice, pulſe, tobacco, and indigo. Here 'are vaſt meadows, which feed large herds 'of great and ſmall cattle; poultry are nume-'rous, as well as wild fowl.' The ſame Author, in his travels to the ſouth of the

river

river *Gambia*, expresses his surprize, 'to see
'the land so well cultivated; scarce a spot
'lay unimproved; the low grounds, divided
'by small canals, were all sowed with rice;
'the higher ground planted with *Indian* corn,
'millet, and peas of different sorts: beef and
'mutton very cheap, as well as all other ne-
'cessaries of life.' The account this Author
gives of the disposition of the natives, is,
'That they are generally good-natured and
'civil, and may be brought to any thing by
'fair and soft means.' *Artus*, speaking of the
same people, says, 'They are a sincere, in-
'offensive people, and do no injustice either
'to one another or strangers.'

From these Accounts, both of the good Disposition of the Natives, and the Fruitfulness of most parts of *Guiney*, which are confirmed by many other Authors, it may well be concluded, that their acquaintance with the *Europeans* would have been a happiness to them, had those last not only bore the name, but indeed been influenced by the Spirit of *Christianity*; but, alas! how hath the Conduct of the Whites contradicted the Precepts and Example of Christ? Instead of promoting the End of his Coming, by preaching the Gospel of Peace and Good-will to Man, they have, by their practices, contributed to enflame every noxious passion of corrupt nature in the Negroes; they have incited them to make war one upon another, and for this purpofe have furnifhed them with prodigious quantities of ammunition and arms, whereby they have been hurried into confufion, bloodfhed, and all the extremities of temporal mifery, which muft neceffarily beget in their minds fuch a general deteftation and fcorn of the *Chriftian* name, as may deeply affect, if not wholly precludo their belief of the great Truths of our holy Religion. Thus an infatiable defire of gain hath become the principal and moving caufe of the moft abominable and dreadful fcene, that was perhaps ever acted upon the face of the earth; even the power of their Kings hath been made fubfervient to anfwer this wicked purpofe, inftead of being Protectors of their people, thefe Rulers, allured by the tempting bait laid before them by the *European* Factors; &c. have invaded the Liberties of their unhappy fubjects, and are become their Oppreffors.

Divers accounts have already appeared in print, declarative of the fhocking wickednefs with which this Trade is carried on; thefe may not have fallen into the hands of fome of my readers, I fhall, therefore, for their information, felect a few of the moft remarkable inftances that I have met with, fhewing the method by which the Trade is commonly managed all along the *African* coaft.

Francis

Francis Moor, Factor to the *African* Company on the river *Gambia*, relates, 'That
' when the King of *Barsalli* wants goods, &c.
' he sends a messenger to the *English* Governor
' at *James*'s Fort, to desire he would send up
' a sloop with a cargo of goods; which (says
' the author) the Governor never fails to do:
' Against the time the vessel arrives, the King
' plunders some of his enemies towns, selling
' the people for such goods as he wants. —
' If he is not at war with any neighbouring
' King, he falls upon one of his own towns,
' and makes bold to sell his own miserable
' subjects.'

N. Brue, in his account of the Trade, &c. writes, 'That having received a quantity of goods, he wrote to the King of the country,
' That if he had a sufficient number of slaves,
' he was ready to trade with him. This
' Prince (says that author) as well as other
' Negroe Monarchs, has always a sure way
' of supplying his deficiencies by selling his
' own subjects. — The King had recourse to
' this method, by seizing three hundred of
' his own people, and sent word to *Brue*,
' that he had the slaves ready to deliver for
' the goods.'

The Misery and Bloodshed, consequent of the Slave-trade, is amply set forth by the following extracts of two voyages to the coast
of

of *Guiney* for flaves. The firft in a veffel from *Liverpool,* taken *verbatim* from the original manufcript of the Surgeon's journal, *viz.*

' SESTRO, *December* the 29th, 1724. No
' trade to-day, though many Traders come
' on board; they inform us, that the people
' are gone to war within land, and will bring
' prifoners enough in two or three days: in
' hopes of which we ftay.

' The 30th. No trade yet, but our Traders
' came on board to-day, and informed us,
' the people had burnt four towns of their
' enemies, fo that to-morrow we expect flaves
' off. Another large fhip is come in: Yefter-
' day came in a large *Londoner.*

' The 31ft. Fair weather, but no trade
' yet: We fee each night towns burning;
' but we hear the *Seftro* men are many of
' them killed by the inland Negroes, fo that
' we fear this war will be unfuccefsful.

' The 2d *January.* Laft night we faw a
' prodigious fire break out about eleven o'
' clock, and this morning fee the town of
' *Seftro* burnt down to the ground, (it con-
' tained fome hundreds of houfes) fo that we
' find their enemies are too hard for them at
' prefent, and confequently our trade fpoiled
' here; fo that about feven o' clock we
weigh'd

' weigh'd anchor, as did likewife the three
' other veffels to proceed lower down.'

The fecond relation, alfo taken from the original manufcript journal of a perfon of credit, who went Surgeon on the fame account in a veffel from *New-York* to the coaft of *Guiney*, about nineteen years paft, is as follows, *viz.*

' Being on the coaft at a place called
' *Bafalia*, the Commander of the veffel, ac-
' cording to cuftom, fent a perfon on fhore
' with a prefent to the King, acquainting
' him with his arrival, and letting him know,
' they wanted a cargo of flaves. The King
' promifed to furnifh them with flaves; and
' in order to do it, fet out to go to war againft
' his enemies, defigning alfo to furprize fome
' town, and take all the people prifoners:
' Some time after, the King fent them word,
' he had not yet met with the defired fuccefs,
' having been twice repulfed, in attempting
' to break up two towns; but that he ftill
' hoped to procure a number of flaves for
' them; and in this defign he perfifted till
' he met his enemies in the field, where a
' battle was fought, which lafted three days;
' during which time the engagement was fo
' bloody, that four thoufand five hundred
' men were flain on the fpot.' The perfon, that wrote the account, beheld the bodies as
they

they lay on the field of battle. 'Think (says he in his journal) what a pitiable fight it was, to see the widows weeping over their lost husbands, orphans deploring the loss of their fathers, &c. &c.'

'Those, who are acquainted with the Trade, agree, that many Negroes on the sea-coast, who have been corrupted by their intercourse and converse with the *European* Factors, have learnt to stick at no act of cruelty for gain. These make it a practice to steal abundance of little Blacks of both sexes, when found on the roads or in the fields, where their parents keep them all day to watch the corn, &c. Some authors say, the Negroe Factors go six or seven hundred miles up the country with goods, bought from the *Europeans*, where markets of men are kept in the same manner as those of beasts with us; when the poor slaves, whether brought from far or near, come to the sea-shore, they are stripped naked, and strictly examined by the *European* Surgeons, both men and women, without the least distinction or modesty; those which are approved as good, are marked with a red-hot iron with the ship's mark; after which they are put on board the vessels, the men being shackled with irons two and two together. Reader, bring the matter home, and consider whether any situation in life can be more completely miserable than that of
those

those distressed captives. When we reflect, that each individual of this number had some tender attachment which was broken by this cruel separation; some parent or wife, who had not an opportunity of mingling tears in a parting embrace; perhaps some infant or aged parent whom his labour was to feed and vigilance protect; themselves under the dreadful apprehension of an unknown perpetual slavery; pent up within the narrow confines of a vessel, sometimes six or seven hundred together, where they lie as close as possible. Under these complicated distresses they are often reduced to a state of desperation, wherein many have leaped into the sea, and have kept themselves under water till they were drowned; others have starved themselves to death, for the prevention whereof some masters of vessels have cut off the legs and arms of a number of those poor desperate creatures, to terrify the rest. Great numbers have also frequently been killed, and some deliberately put to death under the greatest torture, when they have attempted to rise, in order to free themselves from their present misery, and the slavery designed them. An instance of the last kind appears particularly in an account given by the master of a vessel, who brought a cargo of slaves to *Barbadoes*; indeed it appears so irreconcileable to the common dictates of humanity, that one would doubt the truth

D of

of it, had it not been related by a serious person of undoubted credit, who had it from the captain's own mouth. Upon an inquiry, What had been the success of his voyage? he answered, 'That he had found it a diffi‑
'cult matter to set the negroes a fighting
'with each other, in order to procure the
'number he wanted; but that when he had
'obtained this end, and had got his vessel
'filled with slaves, a new difficulty arose
'from their refusal to take food; those de‑
'sperate creatures chusing rather to die with
'hunger, than to be carried from their native
'country.' Upon a farther inquiry, by what means he had prevailed upon them to forego this desperate resolution? he answered,
'That he obliged all the negroes to come
'upon deck, where they persisting in their
'resolution of not taking food, he caused his
'sailors to lay hold upon one of the most
'obstinate, and chopt the poor creature into
'small pieces, forcing some of the others to
'eat a part of the mangled body; withal
'swearing to the survivors, that he would use
'them all, one after the other, in the same
'manner, if they did not consent to eat.'
This horrid execution he applauded as a good act, it having had the desired effect, in bringing them to take food.

A similar case is mentioned in *Astley*'s Collection of Voyages, by *John Atkins*, Sur‑
geon

geon on board Admiral *Ogle*'s squadron, 'Of one *Harding*, master of a vessel, in which several of the men-slaves, and a woman-slave, had attempted to rise, in order to recover their liberty; some of whom the master, of his own authority, sentenced to cruel death; making them first eat the heart and liver of one of those he killed. The woman he hoisted by the thumbs; whipped and flashed with knives before the other slaves, till she died.'

As detestable and shocking as this may appear to such, whose hearts are not yet hardened by the practice of that cruelty, which the love of wealth, by degrees, introduceth into the human mind; it will not be strange to those who have been concerned or employed in the Trade. Now here arises a necessary query to those who hold the ballance and sword of justice; and who must account to God for the use they have made of it. Since our English *law is so truly valuable for its justice*, how can they overlook these barbarous deaths of the unhappy *Africans* without trial, or due proof of their being guilty, of crimes adequate to their punishment? 'Why are those masters of vessels (who are often not the most tender and considerate of men) thus suffered to be the sovereign arbiters of the lives of the miserable Negroes; and allowed, with impunity, thus to destroy, may I not say, murder their

their fellow-creatures, and that by means fo cruel as cannot be even related but with shame and horror.?

When the vessels arrive at their destined port in the Colonies, the poor Negroes are to be disposed of to the planters; and here they are again exposed naked, without any distinction of sexes, to the brutal examination of their purchasers; and this, it may well be judged is to many of them another occasion of deep distress, especially to the females: Add to this, that near connections must now again be separated, to go with their several purchasers: In this melancholy scene Mothers are seen hanging over their Daughters, bedewing their naked breasts with tears, and Daughters clinging to their Parents; not knowing what new stage of distress must follow their separation; or if ever they shall meet again: And here what sympathy, what commiseration are they to expect? why indeed, if they will not separate as readily as their owners think proper, the whipper is called for, and the lash exercised upon their naked bodies, till obliged to part.

Can any human heart, that retains a fellow-feeling for the Sufferings of mankind, be unconcerned at relations of such grievous affliction, to which this oppressed part of our Species are subjected:. God gave to man dominion

dominion over the fish of the sea, and over the fowls of the air, and over the cattle, &c. but imposed no involuntary subjection of one man to another.

The Truth of this Position has of late been clearly set forth by persons of reputation and ability, particularly *George Wallis*, in his System of the Laws of *Scotland*, whose sentiments are so worthy the notice of all considerate persons, that I shall here repeat a part of what he has not long since published, concerning the *African* Trade, *viz*. ' If this ' Trade admits of a moral or a rational justi-
' fication, every crime, even the most attro-
' cious, may be justified: Government was
' instituted for the good of mankind. Kings,
' Princes, Governors, are not proprietors of
' those who are subjected to their authority,
' they have not a right to make them mi-
' serable. On the contrary, their authority is
' vested in them, that they may by the just
' exercise of it, promote the Happiness of
' their people: Of course, they have not a
' right to dispose of their Liberty, and to sell
' them for slaves: Besides, no man has a
' right to acquire or, to purchase them; men
' and their Liberty, are not either saleable or
' purchaseable: One therefore has no body
' but himself to blame, in case he shall
' find himself deprived of a man, whom he
' thought he had, by buying for a price,
                                    ' made

'made his own; for he dealt in a Trade
'which was illicit, and was prohibited by
'the moſt obvious dictates of humanity. For
'theſe reaſons, every one of thoſe unfortunate
'men, who are pretended to be ſlaves, has
'a right to be declared free, for he never
'loſt his Liberty, he could not loſe it; his
'Prince had no power to diſpoſe of him:
'of courſe the ſale was void. This right
'he carries about with him, and is entitled
'every where to get it declared. As ſoon,
'therefore, as he comes into a country, in
'which the Judges are not forgetful of their
'own humanity, it is their duty to remember
'that he is a man, and to declare him to be
'free. — This is the Law of Nature, which
'is obligatory on all men, at all times, and
'in all places. — Would not any of us, who
'ſhould be ſnatched by Pirates from his
'native land, think himſelf cruelly abuſed,
'and at all times intitled to be free? Have
'not theſe unfortunate *Africans*, who meet
'with the ſame cruel fate, the ſame right?
'are not they men as well as we? and have
'they not the ſame ſenſibility? Let us not,
'therefore, defend or ſupport a uſage, which
'is contrary to all the Laws of Humanity.'

Francis Hutchinſon, alſo in his Syſtem of Moral Philoſophy, ſpeaking on the ſubject of Slavery, ſays, 'He who detains another by
'force in ſlavery, is always bound to prove
'his

'his title. The Slave sold or carried away
' into a distant country, must not be obliged
' to prove a negative, that he never forfeited
' his Liberty. The violent possessor must, in
' all cases, shew his title, especially where the
' old proprietor is well known. In this case
' each man is the original proprietor of his
' own Liberty: The proof of his losing it
' must be incumbent on those, who deprived
' him of it by force. Strange, (says the same
' author) that in any nation, where a sense of
' Liberty prevails, where the *Christian* religion
' is professed, custom and high prospect of
' gain can so stupify the consciences of men,
' and all sense of natural justice, that they can
' hear such computation made about the value
' of their fellow-men and their Liberty, with-
' out abhorrence and indignation.'

The noted Baron *Montesquieu* gives it, as his opinion, in his *Spirit of Law*, page 348, ' That nothing more assimilates a man to a
' beast than living amongst freemen, himself
' a slave; such people as these are the natural
' enemies of society, and their number must
' always be dangerous.'

The Author of a pamphlet, lately printed in *London*, entituled, *An Essay in Vindication of the continental Colonies of* America, writes, ' That the bondage we have imposed on the
' *Africans*, is absolutely repugnant to justice.
' That

'That it is highly inconsistent with civil
' policy: First, as it tends to suppress all im-
' provements in arts and sciences; without
' which it is morally impossible that any
' nation should be happy or powerful. Se-
' condly, as it may deprave the minds of the
' freemen; stealing their hearts against the
' laudable feelings of virtue and humanity.
' And, lastly, as it endangers the community
' by the destructive effects of civil commo-
' tions, need I add to these (says that author)
' what every heart, which is not callous to
' all tender feelings, will readily suggest; that
' it is shocking to humanity, violative of every
' generous sentiment, abhorrent utterly from
' the *Christian* Religion: for as *Montesquieu*
' very justly observes, *We must suppose them
' not to be men, or a suspicion would follow that
' we ourselves are not* Christians. —— There
' cannot be a more dangerous maxim, than
' that necessity is a plea for injustice. For
' who shall fix the degree of this necessity?
' What villain so atrocious, who may not
' urge this excuse? or, as *Milton* has happly
' expressed it,

' ——————   —————— *And with necessity
' The tyrant's plea, excuse his dev'lish deed.*

' That our Colonies want people, is a very
' weak argument for so inhuman a violation
' of justice. — Shall a civilized, a *Christian*
' nation encourage Slavery, because the bar-
                                   ' barous

'barous, savage, lawless *African* hath done
'it? Monstrous thought! To what end do
'we profess a religion whose dictates we so
'flagrantly violate? Wherefore have we that
'pattern of goodness and humanity, if we
'refuse to follow it? How long shall we
'continue a practice, which policy rejects,
'justice condemns, and piety dissuades? Shall
'the *Americans* persist in a conduct, which
'cannot be justified; or persevere in oppres-
'sion from which their hearts must recoil?
'If the barbarous *Africans* shall continue to
'enslave each other, let the dæmon slavery
'remain among them, that their crime may
'include its own punishment. Let not *Chri-*
'*stians*, by administring to their wickedness,
'confess their religion to be a useless refine-
'ment, their profession vain, and themselves
'as inhuman as the savages they detest.'

James Foster, in *his Discourses on Natural Religion and Social Virtue*, also shews his just indignation at this wicked practice, which he declares to be *a criminal and outragious violation of the natural right of mankind*. At page 156, 2 vol. he says, 'Should we have read
'concerning the *Greeks* or *Romans* of old, that
'they traded, with view to make slaves of
'their own species, whom they certainly
'knew that this would involve in schemes of
'blood and murder, of destroying or enslaving
'each other, that they even fomented wars,
'and

' and engaged whole nations and tribes in open
' hoſtilities, for their own private advantage;
' that they had no deteſtation of the violence
' and cruelty ; but only feared the ill ſucceſs
' of their inhuman enterpriſes ; that they
' carried men like themſelves, their brethren,
' and the offspring of the ſame common
' parent, to be ſold like beaſts of prey, or
' beaſts of burden, and put them to the ſame
' reproachful trial of their foundneſs, ſtrength
' and capacity for greater bodily ſervice ; that
' quite forgetting and renouncing the original
' dignity of human nature, communicated
' to all, they treated them with more ſeverity
' and ruder diſcipline, than even the ox or
' the aſs, who are void of underſtanding.—
' Should we not, if this had been the caſe,
' have naturally been led to deſpiſe all their
' pretended refinements of morality ; and to
' have concluded, that as they were not
' nations deſtitute of politeneſs, they muſt
' have been *entire Strangers to Virtue and*
' *Benevolence* ?

' But, notwithſtanding this, we ourſelves
' (who profeſs to be *Chriſtians,* and boaſt of
' the peculiar advantage we enjoy, by means
' of an expreſs revelation of our duty from
' Heaven) are in effect, theſe very untaught
' and rude *Heathen* countries. With all our
' ſuperior light, we inſtil into thoſe, whom
' we call ſavage, and barbarous, the moſt
' deſpicable

' defpicable opinion of human nature. We,
' to the utmoft of our power, weaken and
' diffolve the univerfal tie, that binds and
' unites mankind. We practice what we
' fhould exclaim againft, as the utmoft excefs
' of cruelty and tyranny, if nations of the
' world, differing in colour and form of
' government from ourfelves, were fo poffeff-
' ed of empire, as to be able to reduce us to
' a ftate of unmerited and brutifh fervitude.
' Of confequence, we facrifice our reafon, our
' humanity, our *Chriftianity*, to an unnatural
' fordid gain. We teach other nations to
' defpife and trample under foot, all the obli-
' gations of focial virtue. We take the moft
' effectual method to prevent the propagation
' of the Gofpel by reprefenting it as a fcheme
' of power and barbarous oppreffion, and an
' enemy to the natural privileges and rights
' of men.

 ' Perhaps all, that I have now offered, may
' be of very little weight to reftrain this enor-
' mity, this aggravated iniquity. However,
' I fhall ftill have the fatisfaction, of having
' entered my private proteft againft a practice
' which, in my opinion, *bids that God, who*
' *is the God and Father of the* Gentiles, *uncon-*
' *verted to* Chriftianity, *moft daring and bold*
' *defiance, and fpurns at all the principles, both*
' *of natural and revealed Religion.*'

How the *British* nation firſt came to be concerned in a practice, by which the rights and liberties of mankind are ſo violently infringed, and which is ſo oppoſite to the apprehenſions *Engliſhmen* have always had of what natural juſtice requires, is indeed ſurpriſing. It was about the year 1563, in the reign of Queen *Elizabeth,* that the *Engliſh* firſt engaged in the *Guiney* Trade; when it appears, from an account in *Hill*'s Naval Hiſtory, page 293, That when Captain *Hawkins* returned from his firſt voyage to *Africa,* that generous ſpirited Princeſs, attentive to the intereſt of her ſubjects, ſent for the Commander, to whom ſhe expreſſed her concern leſt any of the *African* Negroes ſhould be carried off without their free conſent, *declaring it would be deteſtable, and call down the vengeance of Heaven upon the undertakers.* Captain *Hawkins* promiſed to comply with the Queen's injunction: nevertheleſs, we find in the account, given in the ſame Hiſtory, of *Hawkins*'s ſecond voyage, the author uſing theſe remarkable words, *Here began the horrid practice of forcing the* Africans *into ſlavery.*

Labut, a *Roman* Miſſionary, in his account of the Iſles of *America,* at page 114, of the 4th vol. mentions, that *Lewis* the 13th, Father to the preſent *French* King's Grandfather, was extremely uneaſy at a Law by which all the Negroes of his Colonies were to be made slaves; but it being strongly urged to him, as the readiest means for their Conversion to *Christianity*, he acquiesced therewith.

And altho' we have not many accounts of the impressions which this piratical invasion of the rights of mankind, gave to serious minded people, when first engaged in; yet it did not escape the notice of some, who might be esteemed in a peculiar manner as watchmen in their day to the different societies of *Christians*, whereunto they belonged. *Richard Baxter*, an eminent preacher amongst the *Nonconformists*, in the last century, well known and particularly esteemed by most of the serious *Presbyterians* and *Independents*, in his *Christian* Directory mostly, wrote about an hundred Years ago, fully shews his detestation of this practice in the following words:
' Do you not mark how God hath followed
' you with plagues? And may not conscience
' tell you, that it is for your inhumanity to
' the souls and bodies of men? — To go as
' pirates and catch up poor Negroes, or people
' of another land, that never forfeited Life
' or Liberty, and to make them Slaves and
' sell them, is one of the worst kind of
' Thievery in the world; and such persons
' are to be taken for the common Enemies
' of mankind; and they that buy them, and
' use them as beasts, for their meer com-
' modity,

'modity, and betray, or destroy, or neglect
'their souls, are fitter to be called devils than
'*Christians.* It is an heinous sin to buy them,
'unless it be in charity to deliver them.——
'Undoubtedly they are presently bound to
'deliver them; because by right the man is
'his own; therefore no man else can have
'a just title to him.'

We also find *George Fox*, a man of exemplary piety, who was the principal instrument in gathering the religious society of people called *Quakers*, expressing his concern and fellow-feeling for the bondage of the Negroes: In a discourse taken from his mouth, in *Barbadoes*, in the Year 1671, says, 'Consider with yourselves, if you were in the same
'condition as the Blacks are, — who came
'strangers to you, and were sold to you as
'slaves. I say, if this should be the condition
'of you or yours, you would think it hard
'measure: Yea, and very great bondage and
'cruelty. And, therefore, consider seriously
'of this, and do you for and to them, as
'you would willingly have them, or any
'other to do unto you, were you in the like
'slavish condition; and bring them to know
'the Lord Christ.' And in his journal, page
'431, speaking of the Advice he gave his
'friends at *Barbadoes*, he says, 'I desired also,
'that they would cause their Overseers to deal
'mildly and gently with their Negroes, and
'not

' not to ufe cruelty towards them, as the
' manner of fome had been; and that after
' certain years of fervitude they fhould make
' them free.'

In a book printed in *Liverpool*, called *The* Liverpool *Memorandum-book*, which contains, among other things, an account of the Trade of that port, there is an exact lift of the veffels employed in the *Guiney* Trade, and of the number of Slaves imported in each veffel, by which it appears, that in the year 1753, the number imported to *America*, by veffels belonging to that port, amounted to upwards of Thirty Thoufand; and from the number of Veffels employed by the *African* Company in *London* and *Briftol*, we may, with fome degree of certainty conclude, there is, at leaft, One Hundred Thoufand Negroes purchafed and brought on board our fhips yearly from the coaft of *Africa*, on their account: This is confirmed in *Anderfon's* Hiftory of Trade and Commerce, printed in 1764, where it is faid, at page 68 of the Appendix, ' That *England* fupplies her *American* Colonies with Negro-flaves, amount-
' ing in number to above One Hundred
' Thoufand every year.' When the veffels are full freighted with flaves, they fet out for our plantations in *America*, and may be two or three months on the voyage, during which time, from the filth and ftench that is

among

among them, diftempers frequently break out, which carry off a great many, a fifth, a fourth, yea fometimes a third of them; fo that taking all the flaves together that are brought on board our fhips yearly, one may reafonably fuppofe, that at leaft ten thoufand of them die on the voyage. And in a printed account of the State of the Negroes in our plantations, it is fuppofed that a fourth part, more or lefs, die at the different Iflands, in what is called the feafoning. Hence it may be prefumed, that, at a moderate computation of the flaves, who are purchafed by our *African* merchants in a year, near thirty thoufand die upon the voyage and in the feafoning. Add to this, the prodigious number who are killed in the incurfions and inteftine wars, by which the Negroes procure the number of flaves wanted to load the veffels: How dreadful then is this Slave-Trade, whereby fo many thoufands of our fellow-creatures, free by nature, endued with the fame rational faculties, and called to be heirs of the fame falvation with us, lofe their lives, and are truly, and properly fpeaking, murdered every year! For it is not neceffary, in order to convict a man of murder, to make it appear, that he had an intention to commit murder. Whoever does, by unjuft force or violence, deprive another of his Liberty; and, while he has him in his power, reduces him, by cruel treatment, to fuch a condition as evidently endangers his life,

life, and the event occasions his death, is actually guilty of murder. It is no less shocking to read the accounts given by Sir *Hans Sloan*, and others, of the inhuman and unmerciful treatment those Blacks meet with, who survive the seasoning in the Islands, often for transgressions, to which the punishment they receive bears no proportion. 'And the 'horrid executions, which are frequently 'made there upon discovery of the plots laid 'by the Blacks, for the recovery of their liber-'ty; of some they break the bones, whilst 'alive, on a wheel; others they burn or rather 'roast to death; others they starve to death, 'with a loaf hanging before their mouths.' Thus they are brought to expire, with frightful agonies, in the most horrid tortures. For negligence only they are unmercifully whipped, till their backs are raw, and then pepper and salt is scattered on the wounds to heighten the pain and prevent mortification. Is it not a cause of much sorrow and lamentation, that so many poor creatures should be thus rack'd with excruciating tortures, for crimes which often their tormentors have occasioned: Must not even the common feelings of human nature have suffered some grievous change in those men, to be capable of such horrid cruelty, towards their fellow-men? If they deserve death, ought not their judges, in the death decreed them, always to remember that these

these their hapless fellow-creatures are men, and themselves professing *Christians?* The *Mosaic* law teaches us our duty in these cases, in the merciful provision it made in the punishment of transgressors, *Deuter.* xxv. 2. *And it shall be, if the wicked man be worthy to be beaten, that the judge shall cause him to lie down, and to be beaten before his face, according to his fault, by a certain number; Forty stripes he may give him, and not exceed.* And the reason rendered is out of respect to human nature, *viz. Lest if he should exceed, and beat him above these, with many stripes, then thy Brother should seem vile unto thee.* *Britons* boast themselves to be a generous, humane people, who have a true sense of the importance of Liberty; but is this a true character, whilst that barbarous, savage Slave-Trade, with all its attendant horrors, receives countenance and protection from the Legislature, whereby so many Thousand lives are yearly sacrificed? Do we indeed believe the truths declared in the Gospel? Are we persuaded that the threatnings, as well as the promises therein contained, will have their accomplishment? If indeed we do, must we not tremble to think what a load of guilt lies upon our Nation generally and individually, so far as we in any degree abet or countenance this aggravated iniquity?

We

We have a memorable Instance in history, which may be fruitful of Instruction, if timely and properly applied; it is a quotation made by Sir *John Temple*, in his history of the *Irish* rebellion, being an observation out of *Giraldus Cambrensis*, a noted author, who lived about six hundred years ago, concerning the causes of the prosperity of the *English* undertakings in *Ireland*, when they conquered that Island, he saith, ' That a synod, or
' council of the Clergy, being then assembled
' at *Armagh*, and that point fully debated, it
' was unanimously agreed, that the sins of
' the people were the occasion of that heavy
' judgment then fallen upon their nation; and
' that especially their buying of *Englishmen*
' from merchants and pirates, and detaining
' them under a most miserable hard bondage,
' had caused the Lord, by way of just retali-
' ation, to leave them to be reduced, by
' the *English*, to the same state of slavery.
' Whereupon they made a public act in that
' council, that all the *English*, held in capti-
' vity throughout the whole land, should be
' presently restored to their former Liberty.'

I shall now conclude with an extract from an address of a late author to the merchants, and others, who are concerned in carrying on the *Guiney* Trade; which also, in a great measure, is applicable to others, who, for the

the love of gain, are in any way concerned in promoting or maintaining the captivity of the Negroes.

"As the business you are publickly carrying
'on before the world, has a bad aspect, and
'you are sensible most men make objection
'against it, you ought to justify it to the
'world, upon principles of reason, equity
'and humanity; to make it appear, that it is
'no unjust invasion of the persons, or en‑
'croachments on the rights of men; or for
'ever to lay it aside.— But laying aside the
'resentment of men, which is but of little or
'no moment, in comparison with that of
'the Almighty, think of a future reckon‑
'ing: consider how you shall come off in
'the great and awful Day of accompt. You
'now heap up riches and live in pleasure;
'but, oh! what will you do in the end
'thereof? and that is not far off: what, if
'death should seize upon you, and hurry you
'out of this world, under all that load of
'blood-guiltiness, that now lies upon your
'souls? The gospel expresly declares, that
'thieves and murderers shall not inherit the
'kingdom of God. Consider, that at the
'same time, and by the same means, you
'now treasure up worldly riches, you are
'treasuring up to yourselves wrath, against
'the day of wrath, and vengeance that shall
"come

'come upon the workers of iniquity, unless
'prevented by a timely repentance.

'And what greater iniquity, what crime
'that is more heinous, that carries in it more
'complicated guilt, can you name than that,
'in the habitual, deliberate practice of which
'you now live? How can you lift up your
'guilty eyes to heaven? How can you pray
'for mercy to him that made you, or hope
'for any favour from him that formed you,
'while you go on thus grosly and openly to
'dishonour him, in debasing and destroying
'the nobleft workmanship of his hands in
'this lower world? He is the Father of men;
'and do you think he will not resent such
'treatment of his offspring, whom he hath so
'loved, as to give his only begotten Son, that
'whosoever believeth in him, might not perish,
'but have everlasting life? This love of God
'to man, revealed in the gospel, is a great
'aggravation of your guilt; for if God so
'loved us, we ought also to love one another.
'*You remember the fate of the Servant, who
'took hold of his fellow-servant, who was in his
'debt, by the throat, and cast him into prison:*
'Think then, and tremble to think, what
'will be your fate, who take your fellow-
'servants by the throat, that owe you not a
'penny, and make them prisoners for life.

'Give

' Give yourselves leave to reflect impartially
' upon, and confider the nature of, this Man-
' Trade, which, if you do, your hearts muſt
' needs relent, if you have not loſt all ſenſe
' of humanity, all pity and compaſſion to-
' wards thoſe of your own kind, to think
' what calamities, what havock and deſtruc-
' tion among them, you have been the authors
' of, for filthy lucre's ſake. God grant you
' may be ſenſible of your guilt, and repent in
' time.'

FINIS.

CPSIA information can be obtained
at www.ICGtesting.com
Printed in the USA
LVHW090820161221
706194LV00020B/340